WEATHER WATCH

Fall

by Cynthia Amoroso and Robert B. Noyed

Fall is here! Fall is one of the four **seasons**. Another name for this season is **autumn**. Fall comes after summer and before winter.

Fall is the fourth season of the year.

In the fall, the sun **sets** earlier than it did in the summer. The air is warm during the day and cool at night.

The sun sets over a farm on a fall evening.

The leaves on many trees change color. The leaves turn red, orange, yellow, and brown. Soon the leaves will drop from the trees.

The trees around this lake are turning many colors.

Farmers planted seeds in the spring. In the fall, their crops are ready to **harvest**.

A farmer harvests his crop.

Many plants are done growing in the fall. The vegetables in the garden are ready to pick. The pumpkins have grown large and are bright orange.

Pumpkins are ready to pick in the fall.

Apples are also ready in the fall. They are juicy and colorful. People pick the apples in the **orchards**.

These apples are ready to be picked from the trees.

Fall is a busy time for many animals. They are getting ready for winter. Squirrels gather food to save for winter.

A squirrel stores nuts in the fall.

Many birds are in the sky in the fall. They are flying south for the winter. Some groups of birds make the shape of the letter V as they fly.

Many kinds of birds fly south in the fall.

Leaves cover the ground.
Some people rake the leaves
into piles. Many children love
to jump into the leaves.

A girl jumps into a pile of leaves.

The trees are brightly colored in the fall. The air is crisp. Enjoy the cool weather!

Two sisters play outside in the leaves.

Glossary

autumn (AW-tum): Autumn is another name for fall. Autumn comes after summer.

harvest (HAR-vist): Harvest means to gather a crop on a farm. Farmers harvest in the fall.

orchards (OR-churds): Orchards are farms where fruit grows. Apples grow in orchards.

seasons (SEE-zinz): Seasons are the four parts of the year. The four seasons are winter, spring, summer, and fall.

sets (SETS): The sun sets when it goes below the horizon. The sun sets earlier in the fall than in the summer.

To Find Out More

Books

Branley, Franklyn M. *Sunshine Makes the Seasons*. New York: HarperCollins, 2005.

Roca, Nuria. *Fall*. Hauppauge, NY: Barron's, 2004.

Rockwell, Anne. *Four Seasons Make a Year*. New York: Walker & Co., 2004.

Web Sites

Visit our Web site for links about fall:
childsworld.com/links

Note to Parents, Teachers, and Librarians: We routinely verify our Web links to make sure they are safe and active sites. So encourage your readers to check them out!

Index

air, 4, 20

animals, 14

apples, 12

birds, 16

farming, 8

leaves, 6, 18

summer, 2, 4

sun, 4

trees, 6, 20

vegetables, 10

winter, 2, 14, 16

About the Authors

Cynthia Amoroso has worked as an elementary school teacher and a high school English teacher. Writing children's books is another way for her to share her passion for the written word.

Robert B. Noyed has worked as a newspaper reporter and in the communications department for a Minnesota school district. He enjoys the challenge and accomplishment of writing children's books.

On the cover: Yellow leaves drop from a tree in the fall.

Published by The Child's World®
1980 Lookout Drive • Mankato, MN 56003-1705
800-599-READ • www.childsworld.com

ACKNOWLEDGMENTS
The Child's World®: Mary Berendes, Publishing Director
The Design Lab: Design and production
Red Line Editorial: Editorial direction

PHOTO CREDITS: Lars Lindblad/iStockphoto, cover; iStockphoto, cover, 13, 17, 19; William Walsh/iStockphoto, 3, 7; Iaroslav Danylchenko/ iStockphoto, 5; Steve Mcsweeney/iStockphoto, 9; Eric Simard/ iStockphoto, 11; Stephanie Strathdee/iStockphoto, 15; Christian Carroll/ iStockphoto, 21

Printed in the United States of America in Mankato, Minnesota.
November 2009
F11460

LIBRARY OF CONGRESS CATALOGING-IN-PUBLICATION DATA
Amoroso, Cynthia.
 Fall / by Cynthia Amoroso and Robert B. Noyed.
   p. cm. — (Weather watch)
 Includes index.
 ISBN 978-1-60253-360-8 (library bound : alk. paper)
 1. Autumn—Juvenile literature. I. Noyed, Robert B. II. Title. III. Series.
 QB637.7.A46 2010
 508.2—dc22   2009030212